ashley dun

SMOKE SIGNALS

Smoke Signals
5x8 Second Edition Paperback
978-0-9984381-0-8
Published by Secret Midnight Press
Layout by Jason Turner

www.secretmidnightpress.com
www.ashleydun.com

smoke
signals

(burn this)

Ashley Dun

SMOKE SIGNALS

what you didn't know
is that you handed me
the match
that day you left me with
your words like oil
dripping down
my skin and pooling
at my feet until I'm
drowning in the dark
screaming your name and
what you didn't know
is that your breath
was the heat that
called the spark a flame
until I'm nothing but
a blaze
brief and building
a tower of haze climbing
toward the stars and
what you didn't know
is that now
my dark and greying
glow will
be the one to
guide them
home

the fire.

1.

it's just that
the way your name tastes
in my mouth is like
cotton candy on a hot summer day
melting sugar on my tongue and
it's just that
the rough edges around your fingers
remind me of sand on my skin
foamy tide washing over me and
it's just that
the sun can't stay and
the green leaves are fleeting
and you can't promise me you won't
leave like the summer
and come back resurrected and
our love is a sunset,
a death so beautiful I forget
my sorrow and
it's just that
nothing
lovely
lasts

2.

when you think of me
do you remember the way I
held you when you were a shaking
leaf in a storm
do you remember when I forgave you
every
single
time
and how my love for you stretched
from my soul all the way
around the universe and
back to cradle your heart
do you remember the way I
looked at you in the dim light
damp from dancing in the rain
and the wrinkles by my eyes from
the way we were invincible until
we weren't or until
you chose them over me
do you remember how I
moved on but never let you know
that I remember
every breath and beating and
I hate you for living in the corners of
my mind and I'll never forgive you
for never letting me go

3.

I am drenched in
life and dehydrated from
living
and I can't find
ground to stand on when
I see every life I'm not living
and I am constantly crushed by the
monotony of the life I am
living and I can't even
breathe with this
toxic air of unhappiness
and fear and
each day is our last because
no one will ever know which
breath is our last
so I cry out for meaning
and I dig my fingernails
into the soil because
it's the only thing that's real and
I'm not ready to let go of this
reality because it's all I know and
I'm not ready to give in to
what I don't know so feet
don't fail me now
let's run until the horizon blurs
and the heat of the sun burns
and please
let me die by
the fire
of life

4.

my
mind is
a mine field so
don't wander too far
or the ground will
burst like blood
vessels before
bruises chaos
created by lack
of light
limping through the
dark alleys of
me
lost and
lonely and I beg
you
to keep your distance
safe and sterile and soft
clean and calm you
don't need these burn marks so
march forward through
foot-worn paths far
far away from
me

5.

I heard our song and then
your hands were
on mine
holding them above
my head and
your hot breath on my neck in
mid-summer
fireworks crawling across
the sky outside but
we didn't need anything else to
tell us we were alive as
the record spun like a web
around us and we
thought we
were safe.
I heard our song and then
my hands were
in fists pounding on
your chest
screaming how
how could you leave me like
this like the summer sun
setting in late September like
the smoke from your
cigarettes left a
scent I can never get out

6.

my mind is
melting out of my ears
candle wax dripping under a
flickering fire
and oh how I long for rain

7.

I wish I could
crawl inside your chest
curled up behind your
ribs and tucked between
your lungs I would
swim in the
sea of you.
I wish I could
see through your skull
like a window
and hold your thoughts
in my palms like a
pearl sparkling in
the sunlight.
I wish I could
breathe beauty
through you until
it runs through your
veins like a river and
oh how beautifully
you burn
while I die as the
match that lit you

8.

I spill like
a waterfall
over you
breaking
underneath you
and taking
pieces of you
with me.
I fill like
a well during
a storm when
you breathe
hot fire on my
neck and
it hurts
the way you
land like broken glass
on my back.
I kill like
a starving hunter
in winter
until your
blood runs in
pools with
my own
until I'm still
like a gazelle in the
crosshairs of your
gun
frozen at the
finality of my
fate

9.

there is a bird
bright and beautiful
that lives within me
some days he sings for me
soft and sweet
his melody flows out of me
like rays of light through clouds
some days he sleeps softly
his presence forgotten and I
rest with him
some days he will slowly
stretch his wings
signaling his suffering
I feel his sorrow filling me like
smoke and
some days his cage feels like
it's shrinking and
he lifts his wings
flapping them violently within me
his futile efforts shaking me to the core
and my heart aches for him because
he, like me,
will never be free

CHESHIRE

it can be truly overwhelming
you know
all the lives we're not living
all the paths we're not taking
and the suffocating reality
of the ticking clock
and its irreversible motion
ever forward we
must move unyieldingly
facing life with unbroken breath
or we may miss a moment
in the ice rink of living because
you will slip any second now and it's
over
the lights go black and you are
gone
so how do you possibly accept this
tyranny of time
so vast and yet so inexplicably
irreversible and you are at its whim;
a bet I am unwilling to take
a stake so high I can't possibly fathom
a fully lit life so
let's take every path for
if you don't know where you're going,
"then," said the cat,
"it doesn't matter."

10.

you are the first
sip of coffee
and the last
sip of tea
everything about you
envelopes me

11.

sometimes my brain
crawls into a dusty corner
clawing through the dark and
I think how odd it is that maybe
in the same bed
that I was born in
a person
died.
the same blue scrubs
hovering over his
hollow body in the
same spot that
my existence began and
we both stepped out
screaming.
sometimes my brain
wanders into waters too deep
struggling to breathe and
I think how my life is
as fleeting as a
moth's wing
drawn to the light
not realizing
it's fire and I'm
doused in
gasoline.

12.

I am haunted
your spirit lingers
in between my bones
your voice echoing through
the dark cavities of me
crawling through my
crevices
you whisper all
of the words that
only we knew and
I am haunted
by the smoke after
fireworks on that hot
summer night
by your warm breath whispering
words that ring
painful and shrill in my ears and
long for you
to set me free

the falling.

13.

our love was like hot breath on cold glass
fingers tracing hearts
x's and o's
bodies knotted together in the
back seat of my silver car the
rain coming down on us like
a whisper but all we felt
was fire
eyes full of each other and
our veins were electric as we
swayed like a boat on the waves
as we forgot the beauty of the
dying leaves outside
and for a moment
you were all there was
and for a moment time stopped,
the rain went back into the sky and
the fog cleared
until your name written on the window
disappeared
smoke and vapors like a dream
but I cling onto the mist
hoping you'll miss me again and
I'll be here
waiting for your voice like spring
a sure thing that never
fails to
fail me in
the end

14.

red wine lips and
paint stroke stumbles
wooden warrior
moving through time like
branches in the wind
feel the flowers curl in the cold
fingers frozen buried in pockets
and your soul shrinks
autumn leaves bleed for me
dying for my sins
to be resurrected again
after white death's cool whisper
so close to taking your soul
chilling to the bone
but you know
winter
won't
win

15.

if only
the sky would
swallow me up
making me into
rain drops like
clouds bleeding make
new life
out of nothing
if only
the earth would
crawl up around me
letting me rest
in the dust that I
came from like
mountains always
melt into sand
if only
I could pull apart
putting pieces of myself
in places they fit like
puzzle pieces like
stars scatter
to make constellations
if only
my light would reflect
like sun
rays on stained
glass like mirrors
whisper lies
disguised as truth
telling you
if only

16.

I see the universe when I
close my eyes
nothing but
grey when they're open
each foot in a different world
one weighed down by gravity
and the other floats like
sparkles in the sea
my head lives in the clouds
my feet among the roots of
ancient trees and
my body aches with each
day being pulled between
dreams and reality

17.

your voice is like
honey
dripping down
my throat
but your words like
daggers make me
bleed
so stop
calling my name
in your sleep
because
each cut is curing my
disease of you
draining the illness
of needing you
despite the condition of my
cardiac muscle
every time you
tell me that you
love me because
lord knows
these letters are
lies and
lord knows
I need more
than vows from vowels so please
forgive me and
forget me
while we
sway to the dance of the
devil
while we
weep with each breath
whispering
goodbye

18.

these years like
paint strokes sweep by in
patterns I hadn't imagined.
words like
'tranquilizers' are
triggers and the smell of
smoke takes me
to you.
my thoughts fill my head like
water and I'm
drowning in
your goodbye.

dearest binx,

when you hug me, you hold my head close to your chest. there are ways in which you are perfectly wrong for me. this is not one of them. you send me notes in the early morning while I dream, before the sun rises. these words form the string that wraps me around your finger. despite the broken lines that create our connection, the list of don'ts that apply to you, my thoughts drift often to you. my heart should not be this magnetic.

I look into the mirror and see a shadow of a person; a vague, dark silhouette, longing to be filled in and made whole. when will this fog clear? my energy is waning like the winter sun. I am at a crossroads, but the clouds are low and dense. this grey, milky sky is making my vision dim, disguising my options to make at this fork in the road.

is it obvious to you my fear of falling in love? perhaps I'm confused, blinded by this fog, by you. can you hear my heart breaking? maybe last night you heard the sound like standing on ice in early spring. maybe you sensed the changing of the seasons when we first met.

is it too late for us? how many times can I say I'm sorry before the scars start to fade? my broken heart is leaving a trail of of wounds in its wake, and I am in your debt.

love,
bambi

19.

one year has passed
since you buried yourself in
my soul
made a home underneath my skin
and even though you're gone
you've left behind pieces of your
shrapnel from the war and
it hurts when I move a certain way
your remnants dig into my flesh
and a flash
a picture of you blinds me and
I'm broken down again
you left your pieces and
you took some of mine with
you and
I will never be the same

20.

maybe it wasn't for us
you know
this life
the one where sunrises and
sunsets are so beautiful it
hurts like the razor edge of a
snowflake and
maybe it wasn't for us
the strings of the violin that
vibrate in the softest way to melt
our hearts but
despite the songs you
sang me
the poems you wrote me
the hands on the clock moved in
such a way to call us
elsewhere
away from one another
though it hurts but
in the end
maybe it wasn't for us
the way our skin bonded like
hot metal to plastic
broken pieces of glass
into art
light glowing through it but
maybe it wasn't for us
this life
so I'll be the
one in red
waiting
in the next

21.

when you look at me
I feel the freckles of your eyes
like shadows repelling the
sun from my skin
and when you say my name
I feel the letters wrap around me
like barbed wire and
when you hold her it's like
a hot shower on a cold day
singeing the feeling from my skin
fiery release
I burn at the stake so that you
can be free

22.

oh it hurts
I read these words
that I spewed out like
sewage and
oh I'm sick
my soul looks like
the flowers you gave me
weeks ago and like
the words you wrote me
months ago that once meant
something and now
the shapes of the letters are
cold like coffins
flowerbeds in fall
and all I need is for you to
not need me and
all I want is for you to
want me

23.

is this what living looks like?
like there's this gaping
wound in my chest
like salt water
washed over it and
breathing is more like
gasping and
this can't be what living looks like.
like the night never ends
and the stars have been
eaten alive by
the black sky and
I'll never know
why the sun never seems
to rise in the places my
eyes look upon through
broken glasses.
this won't be what living looks like.
I will sew up my shattered
spirit with twine and
I will
be my own light.
I will
be a spark to
ignite the sun and
defeat the
cold dark of night.

24.

do you ever get tired of communicating?
like it's pulling teeth and each
tooth is a precious gem to
you like
it's giving birth
but you didn't choose to
hurt like this to
be born in the first place and
recreating is just
shedding skin
till you're raw and new
but still
no one sees you
the way you
long to be seen.
do you ever get tired of communicating?
because words will never
suffice for the
hurricane of
feelings for the
tornado of   cure the sickness of
bleeding you feel   language the disease
inside of you constantly   of desire to
swirling in your   shed your skin to
milky way mind but   be truly seen to
all they see are   be truly heard.
raindrops on silky   do you ever get tired of communicating?
sea water while the
rest of you spins on into eternity
because communicating
can never

25.

my fragile frame can barely
stand the changing winds
chilling each bone like
icy fingertips on the tongue
and it hurts to breathe
but you wouldn't know that
by my white teeth
though the shape of my back
suggests the weight I am carrying
the cross I am bearing
both your sins and mine
and you've left me with them all
while the breeze whispers your name
and my dreams haunt me with
my eyes open and closed

the dark.

26.

my fingernails
are filled
with dirt from
trying to
climb out of
the grave you
gave me
that day you
took my breath
without
returning it

27.

for a moment I thought
the sky was whispering
sweet secrets to soothe
my scarred soul
the outlines of the clouds like
mountains make me
feel renewed and
for a moment I thought
I would be okay like
the light blue loved me
more than I ever could until
I blinked my heavy
eyelids and the blue turned
black

28.

strange
how two souls connect
can weave into each other
a tapestry of memory
songs and silhouettes
taste and touch
melt into one bleeding
ink sketch dripping with
salt water seared into
your thoughts until you breathe
your final breath
these two separate souls
heart beats stagger and split
flesh on flesh
scream sorrow as the cords
drop and fray
slow motion walk away
hollowness left where this
once intimate creature held
you close is now nothing but a
stranger.

29.

your lips leave a taste like
metal on mine
that dull taste of
blood
and I can't stop
tonguing the wound
a pain so familiar
so intimate
and I'd rather feel
this ache than
nothing at all
but oh god you hold me like
a cocoon and I am
transformed
set free and
your embrace
tastes like the
sunrise after
a storm
but if you could only see
the power
you have over me
you would feel the ground
shaking beneath me and the
sky weighing down on me
like a stone
and oh god how I wish I felt
nothing at all

30.

today
I painted the town red
and it splattered in lines
across my wrists
while I sacrifice myself
at the altar of
my culture
raging against the bright
fire of life
swallowing my soul
until all that remains
is smoke and
I break like
hot glass under cold water
when I reach out
further than my soul can stretch
so instead I dig in
fingers in the dirt so
my veins feed into the
roots and I am
healed from this
shattered system that
slices through the core
of me while I
bleed out the
red sickness of being until
I am finally
free

31.

when you say my name
I see the letters trickling
off your lips like
blood
spilling out of you like
a sickness
and I'm so
sorry
for calling you
cursed like
anyone who has
looked at me with
hungry eyes
will never
leave satisfied

32.

I live in a cage
of language and longing
flowers trying to bloom
in a dark dry corner
fire in a volcano that
will never erupt
and the stars laugh
never letting me feel them
they're bright but not blinding
beautiful but distant
and I understand them
watching the world from afar
words failing me
my heart betraying me
I'm banging against these walls
but my fists hurt from fighting it
there's no key that will unlock my misery
so I wait
for life to escape me
my spirit set free from feeling

IN CASE YOU WERE WONDERING

depression is like trying to roll up a hill

while the rocks are rolling down.

33.

the world has lost its color
greens and blues sucked from
the veins it is now
pale and lifeless
cold, unwelcoming
small cracks split my skin and
joy seeps out
I have lost my color
bones like ice
sharp and jagged
I fear myself
what I will become
when I thaw

34.

it hurts too much
the glow is dim and
the fire failing
I am thirsty for life
my eyes hunger and my
flesh longs for discovery
introspective inspiration
and an explosion of emotion
I won't settle for the cracks
in this land the filthy features
of my surroundings
surrendering to
the inevitable and I am
incapable of healing
without change and
god I need your fix and I'm
broken without your breath in
my lungs

35.

how many
shades of blue
do you see when I speak
when I close my eyes
the tides sigh around me
the skies cry tears like
water on words
blurring ink
black dripping
down to my heels
blood before it leaves my
veins showing through
my weary flesh my
shades of blue
are calming to you
but you can't see how my
shades of blue
are slowly killing me

36.

my thoughts swirl around me
wrapping me up with their
barbed wire and
I'm bleeding words
hot emotion oozing and
pooling at my feet and
no one can see it
only I am left here to
drown in the poison
I created for myself;
a subtle suicide
for the paralyzed poet.

37.

it's like a snake has been
slithering up my spine
since birth
slowly wrapping its silky body
around mine, numbing
and tonguing my spirit like
a morning frost.
shiny black
burning cold to the
touch but
I've lost the feeling
in my fingers so
I know that I'm
numb and somehow the
chill is welcome
calling me into the quiet
blackness
binding me in its
coils whispering
it'll be over soon
it'll be over soon

38.

I feel like I'm crawling
in an endless dark I'm on
black gravel and my
bleeding palms pull me
forward into the neon night.
the air is heavy,
there is nothing before me so I
could curl up in
the cracked earth or I
could skid my skin across
these crude rocks and I'm
not sure I will survive and I'm
not sure I want to

MY HAND

this is for when you crave the burn
like swallowing
singes your insides like
black coals with orange outlines
like it hurts until
it can't anymore until
scars cover your skin like scales as
a dark armor for the fire.
this is for when you crave the burn
like a raging river
runs through your veins
pulling you like claws
into the grave but
you need it
more than breathing
more than bleeding
because hurting is healing.
this is for when you crave the burn
when all you want
is to let the sorrow
swallow you please
take this like a life raft
and please
never let it go.

39.

sometimes it hurts
to put these words on
the page like
an amputation
from my brain
pieces of my soul
       falling out like
  raindrops until I
no longer
exist

40.

what happens to the words
'I love you'
once they've spilled out
of your mouth like
that time we rolled down
the soft green hill
laughing and our
bruises became
landmarks like
grass stains will
always remind me of
those hot summer days
with you and ever since
you said those words
it's like they floated off with
the smoke from your cigarette so
how can I hold onto them
turning them into soft clay in my
hands to mold with
warmth and make them
mean something again

41.

I drink darkness like
ink
spills slowly through
my veins until
I bleed black and
its silky sorrow
weaving a web
fills each fiber
with weight like
iron and shapes
like shackles
surround each strand
of my DNA
pulling me six
feet underground but
I know I am
stronger than your
secret syringes
stealing life from
my veins until
my flesh turns to earth so
until then I will
fight
against the darkness like
a sunrise
shattering night and
even when it seems like the
black is burying me
I will rise
with the
spring roses
out of snow

the rebirth.

42.

you are the sun breaking
through drawn blinds strewn
across these walls dancing
through veiny leaves embracing
every inch of my being
and you call me whole
you ignite the moon keeping
me from utter darkness guiding
me through the night like
a ship in a storm pulling
me into your arms
and I call you home

43.

never get comfortable with mental illness
it is not your friend
it is a force you must fight
I know the heat is like home
burning embers on your flesh and
you know you're alive but
you can't let it consume
all the crevices of you because
there is life where water runs
cool across your feet
rapid and royal it
breathes life into your bones
unlike this smoke that smothers you
like wool on a warm night.
never get comfortable with mental illness
or it'll steal your soul when
you least suspect it so
seek the light
brave like morning
bursting through darkness and
hold on for the new
if the sun can do it
so can you.

44.

it's like I woke up one morning broken
my porcelain shattered and
I sewed up my skin like
silk but it never looked
the same.
it's like I woke up one morning boring
my bright dulled and my
petals wilted
like I'm a drawing that's been
erased
a shadow of me left
pieces swept away in the wind.
it's like I woke up one morning bleeding
it leaks out of me like lava
a burning blessing
and each day I'm deflating
oxygen sneaking out until
I'm nothing but for now
I will wake up each morning bolder
brought to life by the light
and like a wildflower in winter
I will always fight

45.

what if I don't live to be
ninety
but oh god
what if I do?
do I want to see the world through
weary eyes
death sleeping next to me
and life seeping out of the cracks?
I feel the weight of
each second
like a boulder burying me so
instead of having
ninety
years I hope to have
ninety
scars from tumbling down mountains and
ninety
thousand freckles from sun kisses and
ninety
dreams blossomed into gardens
but despite the minutes of my
feet on the earth I know that
each second
ninety
million nerve endings are firing so that
my lungs can rise again and
I'm holding on like
each second
is my savior so
what if I don't live to be
ninety
but oh god
what if I do?

46.

I am woman
I am wonder-filled.

I am a mountain range
speckled with snow
standing strong against
your elements.
I rage like
salt water in a storm,
carrying you
on my back like
bricks but
I am soft enough to
drown you.

I am woman
I am wonder-filled.

47.

it's wild how the older you get,
the more you see and experience -
the smaller your mind gets.
it's as though it is afraid of wondering,
afraid of the outcome of curiosity because
it has wandered into fire before.
it hurts that I used to feel so much more;
to be changed by art once and
now my soul is frigid and afraid.
how do I stay malleable and
yet strong against the tenacious heat of reality?
if only my spirit would melt in the hot sun,
liquid gold to be stirred and
always glistening in the movement of being.
but instead brick walls are built around it so
I feel nothing.
I protect myself so much that I am empty and
I ache for this.
is it freedom to feel?
should I live each moment like a meteor,
bright and blazing on a constant current
though I know I will burn out in the end?
these questions haunt me with each burst
of blood from my vessels because
what else matters besides being?
as I slowly decay my spirit rages on with
each breath whispering,
"Be."

48.

sometimes I feel like
I could just dig into my skin
and slowly peel it back until
my true form emerges
like this shell of flesh is a
straight jacket holding me
until I go numb from fighting it
like my heartbeat could just
shatter my frame if it felt like it
my fragile corpse swaying
in the wind and my tiny soul
flickers like a flame at
the end of a burned match.
sometimes I feel like
minutes are just the
grains of dirt that fill the
hole you're buried in.
sometimes I feel like
my feelings could be
the sickness or
the cure and what
kills me is that I'll
never know the
difference

49.

if I die young
don't weep for me.
I have lived
a life overflowing.
I have seen the world
I have known sweet souls
I have known love
sweeter than the
summer sun.

if I die young
don't bury me
in a cemetery.
I am no longer here so
turn my body into
a tree of life.
you can sit beneath the shade,
breathe deeper as its offspring
keep the time of the seasons
of your own life and remember -

life is precious
life is beautiful
life is yours.

50.

this heart is tiny and timid but
its beat makes the floors shake and the
drums in your ears pulse and you
feel the blood flowing
quickly through your veins and you
put your hand to your chest because
god, life is a cobweb in the wind
and this beating is the only thing
keeping your feet on the ground so
don't grab onto the clouds but
watch them with wonder as your
eyelids flutter with
the shaking leaves and let your soul
grow into the earth like roots
so the thumping in your chest will feel
more like fireworks than a
firing squad and I promise
there is healing where the hurt was
hope where the heart broke and
every day on this side of the earth is
worth it

51.

we held hands in the sun walking through the streets where I was raised. I made a home for you in a quiet corner of my heart. I filled it with colorful tapestries, candles that smell like innocence, and music that floats like a cool breeze through you. we walked on the moon and the glow beneath us ignited courage in our hearts. the stars covered us in sparkling beauty, a gentle blanket in a cold reality. we laid our bodies on the earth while the sky spilled autumn leaves around us. there was no separation between our souls and creation, a colorful curiosity stirring inside of us. the pouring rain engulfed us as we sat motionless. the cleansing water told us we were free. our spirits lifted and danced with the rain that day and we knew. without saying words we always know. hearts like ours are soft like clay but bright as diamonds. I made a home for you in a quiet corner of my heart. this home is safe and soft, a nest for you to rest. stay as long as you need.

52.

there's this
beating in my chest
that belonged to you
as the leaves were born on barren branches
your name bloomed within me and
created a home there
you were a cherry blossom
and I inhaled your scent like
a healing breath
I saw the sky alive in your eyes and felt
my heart like a hummingbird
and without warning
your petals wilted and fell around me
leaving me with a withered memory
a hope so temporary and every day
I see the tree you lived on that is now
flowerless but I know like spring
love will always return
it will heal this heart in pieces like petals
and the promise of cherry blossoms
makes me whole
as I call this
beating in my chest
my own

53.

I've lost discernment between dream and reality.
I saw your back facing me but
maybe I didn't.
you turned to face me and your eyes
told me the story of your emptiness.
you kissed my cheek and
walked over the edge of the cliff.

I saw my heart breaking before me but
maybe I didn't.
it was beating, beating, beating
to the rhythm of our song and
I thought I smelled your scent.
tear-stained pillows are all that
remain from that damp, warm night.
I can barely remember the shape of your
ears or the texture of your hands but
your voice sings a painful melody in my ears.

I saw an old piano in a forgotten room but
maybe I didn't.
a woman I saw at the train station appeared and sat at the
bench.
she laid her head on the keys in defeat.
the chords moan and split
playing the song of her heartache.

I've lost discernment between dream and reality.
I'm seeing myself now but
maybe I'm not.
I walk toward the woman and whisper in her ear:

...contd

....

the sun rises and falls
like your lungs in perfect harmony.
five senses,
four limbs,
three freckles in constellation,
two eyes and
one heart sending blood in circulation
like the earth around the sun.
remember:
'I am alive."

54.

broken
blind
bleeding
but still
feeling
and I will wait
patiently for
spring to
save me

55.

when I wrote down those words
black ink cutting through
clean paper
pen piercing the
snowy page
I was thinking of you.
when I took that photo
my plum lips curled like twine tied
them to the secrets twirled in
my hair and
I was thinking of you.
when my sharp inhale caught me
with my fingers
covering my gaping lips
as the sun dripped down the sky like
a glowing pink popsicle
I was thinking of you.
and if you must know
as I lift my chest
inhaling another moment into my
brief existence
I lick my lips and
lock my eyelids and as
each little flutter of being
goes by
I am thinking of you.

56.

our love is
like the crescent moon
carrying me in
its craters and
cutting me with
its edges
breaking me at
the bow and
singing me to sleep at
the stern we
sway with the
stars in the
milky night
and melt when
morning
comes

57.

a happy poem:
I forget.

58.

break the beat
taste the scream rising
from your toes and
fluttering in your lungs like
a magician's dove appearing from
darkness

flicker and wave
let the heat of life devour you
melting like wax
as a beautiful
fiery
avalanche

colorful courage
flowers flow through your veins
and your spirit stretches
and groans like the
trees in a windstorm

feel it all
orange and white
burn your skin
life is full of you
and the stars burn
bright and blazing
even in the
darkest blue

59.

she unfolds before you like
pages in your favorite
book like
a blazing rose in spring
and you ache for her
longing to discover
the rhythm in her breath
the pattern her eyelashes flutter as
they send chills through your skin like
ocean waves and you gaze
at her spirit
as it sparkles like
stars in the velvet night

60.

I am free
despite what my mind tells me
oxygen flows like a gentle breeze
through mountain top trees
and my limbs are strong like
giant pines
full of life and seeping the sap of
righteousness
fighting through the seasons
endless patience and
silent wisdom
I am free
despite what you tell me
my heart stomps through
muddy trenches
and the rain floods my veins
and no one
can take
my freedom
from me